Re:CONSIDERING

ACHIEVEMENT ADDICTION

Justine Toh

I0163034

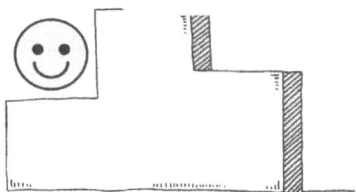

a. Acorn Press

Published by Acorn Press, an imprint of Bible Society
Australia, in partnership with the Centre for Public
Christianity.
ACN 127 775 973
GPO Box 4161
Sydney NSW 2001
Australia
www.publicchristianity.org

ISBN 9780647531327 (pbk); 9780647531334 (ebk)

NATIONAL
LIBRARY
OF AUSTRALIA

A catalogue record for this
book is available from the
National Library of Australia

Editor: Kristin Argall
Cover and text design: John Healy
Text layout:Wes Selwood

About the Centre for Public Christianity

What is the good life?
What does it mean to be human?
Where can I find meaning?
Who can I trust?

In sceptical and polarised times, the Centre for Public Christianity (CPX) seeks to engage the public with a clear, balanced, and surprising picture of the Christian faith. A not-for-profit media company, since 2007 CPX has been joining the dots between contemporary culture and the enduring story of Jesus in the articles, podcasts, books, documentaries, and other resources we produce.

We believe Christianity still has something vital to say about life's biggest questions. Find out more about our team and the work we do at www.publicchristianity.org or follow us on Facebook, Twitter, and Instagram.

CPX CENTRE FOR PUBLIC CHRISTIANITY

About the author

Justine Toh is Senior Fellow at the Centre for Public Christianity, where she speaks and writes about the Christian faith in publications like *The Sydney Morning Herald*, *The Canberra Times*, *The Spectator*, and ABC *Religion & Ethics*. She occasionally guest hosts ABC Radio National's *God Forbid*, a panel program exploring contemporary religion, and has co-presented the documentary *For the Love of God: How the church is better and worse than you ever imagined*. Justine has a PhD in Cultural Studies from Macquarie University in Sydney and tweets, erratically, at @justinetoh. And yes, she is a recovering achievement addict.

CONTENTS

INTRODUCTION 1
   The 'addict' label 2
   Worshipping success 4
   The crack house of achievement addiction 6
   My fog of shame 8

1. STRIVE 11
   An ambush of tigers 13
   Everyone is a concerted cultivator 16
   Everyone is kind of Asian now 19

2. SUFFER. 23
   Pleasure-pain projects 25
   Work as salvation 30
   A lonely girl 33

3. SMUG 36
   A modern fairytale 38
   'Deplorables' 41
   The world according to Ravenclaw 44
   It's not about everyone getting a trophy 47

4. STORY TIME 49
   Write your own deliverance 50
   Meritocracy meets its match 52
   Beloved community 56
   What luck to be alive 58

CODA. 61

NOTES 63

For pretty much every woman I know.

Re:CONSIDERING

INTRODUCTION

I've long known that achievement is my kind of alcohol.

For me, nothing else delivers quite the same high as *getting things done* – and done really, really well. I may have finished school a long time ago but I never really left, if you know what I mean.

Yet, I often forget/lie to myself about my achievement addiction. So it's a good thing that there are plenty of ordinary, everyday moments to remind me of the bleeding obvious: that compulsive behaviour migrating from one area of life to another is the MO of an addict.

Like the way I drive my car.

It's a hybrid with a console that helpfully diagrams when the car wheels are charging the electric battery and when the engine – which runs on fuel – kicks in to give the car more grunt. It's a simple system: green arrows from the wheels to the battery are storing energy; red or yellow arrows from the battery and engine to the wheels are using it.

All those years spent studying, it turns out, have settled deep into my soul, leaving me compelled to ace all the non-tests of life.

In this case, by driving in a way that means I never

have to buy petrol again. My eyes zigzag between the road and the screen, trying to find the sweet spot where I can coast along indefinitely, powered by nothing but my sustainably electric battery and the feel-good fumes of my self-regard.

Call it hybrid hubris.

I don't wind up crashing the car – this is no fable with ready-made moral. My husband just realised what I was doing and turned off the screen.

But I could have crashed, because I was so distracted. So let my near-brush with not-quite-death serve as a cautionary tale: achievement addiction may not (usually) be fatal, but it's still no way to live.

The 'addict' label

In outing myself as an achievement addict, I must admit that I lack the résumé to prove it: one stacked with references to global centres of power and influence like Google, the UN, Harvard, Goldman Sachs, the World Bank, Tik Tok. I have no social-media presence commanding the attention of millions. I've never run a marathon, given a TED talk, been awarded the university medal, authored a bestseller, or made sourdough, like, *ever*.

But you don't need that kind of résumé to be an achievement addict. If any of your devices have more than 20 browser tabs open at any one time, you probably are one. If someone tells you you've done a good job and you feel an intense ripple of pleasure through your soul, then you definitely are one. The same goes if you daydream about work or your personal goals. Or if you find yourself a little bit too impressed – or, at the other end, rather snobbish – at finding out what someone does for a living. You probably know all the reasons you shouldn't measure the value of a life by someone's achievements – and yet here you are: an addict.

I get that the 'addict' label is a gut punch – suggesting, as it does, a disordered, insatiable appetite – in this case, for approval. Plus, we don't normally associate achievement with addiction, because surely we can only be addicted to substances, like drugs?

But addiction may be just as much a spiritual affliction as a medical condition. As Carl Jung once observed of an alcoholic and former patient: 'His craving for alcohol was the equivalent, on a low level, of the spiritual thirst of our being for wholeness, expressed in medieval language: the union with God.' For good measure, Jung stuck a Bible verse in a footnote: 'As the deer pants for streams of water, so my soul pants for you, my God' (Psalm 42:1).

The addict, Jung suggests, genuinely yearns for God, the source of all satisfaction. But addiction warps that spiritual longing by becoming a substitute god. A particularly punishing one, in fact, since addiction constricts your focus so that you're willing to sacrifice everything for your next high. But the more you give of yourself to this counterfeit god, the more it takes and it takes and it takes and never delivers lasting fulfilment.

This is why AA gets its recovering alcoholics to resist the drink by appealing to a higher power – God, or if that's not your thing, whatever gives you meaning and purpose. As Jung would have said: 'spiritus contra spiritum' – meaning spiritual practice must counter alcoholic spirits. You can only fight one god with another.

That's the battle we'll be waging – all in good time.

Worshipping success

Maybe you're not an alcoholic, or convinced that you've a spiritual itch that only God can scratch. But you probably have a dysfunctional relationship with achievement. How could you not? We live in a world that worships hard-won success.

Take Australia's fixation with winning gold medals at the Olympics – and the greater the odds the athlete has overcome to get themselves to that point, the sweeter the victory. Or who can resist the lure of a good Before-and-After shot: photographic proof of someone's discipline, commitment and, as a result, triumphant victory over the flab.

Or ask journalist Barbara Ehrenreich, who wrote an exposé on the way positive thinking gets pushed as an unofficial cure for cancer – which subtly implies that someone's failure to go into remission is *their* fault. In a similar vein, see also Rhonda Byrne's self-help sensation *The Secret*, which advised vision boards to attract health, wealth, husband, and house into your life. If you want these badly enough, the thinking goes, use the power of attraction to manifest them into existence.

Or consider competitive reality-TV shows, and the way that contestants are forced to plead their case before judges to avoid elimination. Regardless of whether this is *Masterchef/Project Runway/The Biggest Loser*, contestants all say some version of the same thing: 'I want this so badly. I'll work so hard. I've got so much more to show you.' In other words, they'll prove through their hard work and effort that they deserve to remain in the competition where, apparently, the one who tries hardest wins.

And what about performance management tools like the 9-Box Grid? One friend tells me that at work she gets 'talent-mapped' on an x-y scale, where x measures performance and y measures potential. The most coveted spot is in the high-performing/high-potential box labelled 'star', which puts the employee on track for promotions and pay rises. But if the employee is judged low performing/low potential, they risk being 'managed out' of the company. Yes, this is *The Hunger Games* of the corporate world, where everyone is striving to be Katniss Everdeen – but someone has to end up in the position of dead meat (ok, just fired).

Even the way we mark significant life milestones seems achievement obsessed, reports *The Sydney Morning Herald*. Trading in one's spouse for a trophy wife being such a Boomer thing to do, Gen-X mid-life crises apparently just settle for the trophy instead: through running a marathon, or trekking to Everest Base Camp. Pursuing any activity, really, that emphasises high performance, self-mastery, and the ability to transform our bodies.

Consider, also, the charged rhetoric of former Australian Treasurer Joe Hockey upon handing down the federal budget in 2014. 'We are a nation of lifters, not leaners', Hockey declared. 'By everyone making a contribution now, we will build a bigger, better Australia.' Hence, among other measures, the budget's proposed long wait times for unemployment benefits and Work for the Dole schemes to wean young people off the government teat.

In praising self-reliant 'lifters' as ideal Australian citizens, Hockey chided those who relied on the public purse. It was a message that conveyed, contra that feel-good golden oldie: *try not to lean on me when you're not strong. I'll resent being your friend. I'll grudgingly help you carry on.* Not quite as catchy as the original.

The crack house of achievement addiction

All these stories celebrate achievement, as well as the idea that we earn, through our effort and hard work, whatever success comes our way. This notion goes by various guises. Input equals output. You get what you deserve. Hard work pays off. You can make something of yourself.

It's the American Dream – although given how

pervasive this idea is, it's not only Americans who dream it. Which means that our addiction to achievement can't be disentangled from the fact that we live in a meritocracy.

A meritocratic system is one that distributes rewards and success on the basis of hard work and deservingness – not riches, rank, or any other inherited privilege. In contrast to an aristocracy, a meritocracy advances a vision of social mobility and equal opportunity.

We'll explore the idea of meritocracy further in Chapter 3. But for now, let's just note that we generally operate with a meritocratic mentality, one that goes by the formula:

hard work + perseverance =
success you have rightly earned

We have all internalised this mentality to some extent, because none of us could avoid ground zero of meritocratic striving. Or, if you like, the crack house of achievement addiction: school.

In our tender years, we were subject to endless drills and assessments, and having our performance measured against that of our peers. All the group work, butcher's paper brainstorming sessions, late-night cramming, essays, exams, projects, quizzes, performances, presentation-day awards, report cards, teacher-parent evenings, all the stressing, stressing, stressing.

For some kids, jumping through those seemingly endless hoops of school life is just a rite of passage. One you graduate from when you finish school.

Others find themselves harshly judged by the reigning standards of academic success, and check out of the system in one way or another. You have students consoling themselves that something else is their thing: sport, dance, music. Other kids resort to mucking around in class because they can't make sense of the work. Or they've got too much else happening in their young lives to focus on school.

Then there's people like me, for whom accumulating gold stars became an unwitting index of self-worth.

My fog of shame

I was destined to become addicted to achievement. Among my people, 'this is the way', as they say in *The Mandalorian*.

When I say 'my people' I mean, of course, Chinese migrants and their browbeaten offspring, for whom admission to a selective public high school is both a deeply coveted prize and an unofficial on-ramp to Future Glory.

When I was 10 years old, my older sister secured her place in posterity with her admission to a selective school. She was also a passionate and accomplished piano player, and I'd thus far proven very average at that pursuit. (Yes, along the way we'll touch on several clichés of Asian parenting – in this case, an insistence on learning a musical instrument.) So, following in her schooling steps was crucial.

You have to get into that school, my parents demanded. *Otherwise, we'll worry about you.* A little line, but it sank like a stone to the bottom of my soul. At my house, 'worry' is a well-known synonym of 'despair', and it was clear they already held grave fears for my future success if I didn't clear this particular hoop.

I didn't.

The next six years passed in a fog of shame. I would like to tell you that I rebelled. But my adolescent self was frantically striving because I believed that the quality of my work was directly tied to my worth.

Ferocious study followed, driven by two parts love of the learning, three parts fear of failure. I loved my friends and my public school. But I see now that there were times that I didn't rate the feedback my teachers gave me – and all because I didn't attend a selective school. It didn't matter if I topped my classes. You'd still be a bottom feeder in *that* school, I'd sternly tell myself.

Yeah, I was *soooo* fun to be around. Like the time I told a girl in Year 12 Modern History that her disengagement with school would drag down everyone's marks in the final exams (and yes, in saying 'everyone', everyone knows I really meant mine).

Oh the irony. The quirks of family and fate had made me the perfect student: copious note-taker, general eager beaver. The one the teacher called upon when the class was dead silent.

But looking back, I could also rattle off the harms of being reduced to a league table of merits and demerits. Being made in that injurious image is one thing; paying the insult forward to someone else is another. Treat someone like that – especially when you know better – and all the straight A's in the world can't compensate for the fact that you've flunked life.

A tree is known by its fruits, goes the proverb. If you treat people as though they're the sum of their achievements, prepare for them to *strive* endlessly, *suffer* along the way, and be *smug* when they prosper. Which isn't as pithy as a proverb, but is perfectly honest nonetheless. And this just happens to be our itinerary for exploring the effects of our shared achievement addiction.

Let me explain.

1. STRIVE

Work ethic-wise, I peaked at 18. To prepare for my final high-school exams, I spent weekends writing essays under exam conditions. Afterwards, my hand would be a claw, the jagged shapes of letters evidence of the physical strain – and maybe my fraying mental state. But I'd feel less haunted than before I picked up the pen. Even, strangely, high.

I can barely remember what I wrote about, but I can't shake what all that practice taught me: the need – nay, the compulsion – to work, work, work: to prove myself, to justify my existence. All in the hope that one day, all that strenuous effort would pay off.

But reading about the study habits of high achievers today, it hits me: *I got off light.*

Take 15-year-old Tina Huang, who told novelist Alice Pung that she sat a three-hour scholarship preparation test *every week* at her coaching college. Maths, English, and two essays were routinely covered, though 'for an extra $25 you could also do an abstract-reasoning test', Huang said. 'They run the tests through a machine and *tah-dah*, you have your results and self-worth all summed up in a pretty blue graph.'

Exam prep *and* excoriating self-examination.

Asians do love a bargain!

Then there's a certain hall at Sydney's Olympic Park where, these days, academic striving has superseded athletic ambition. In summer, when teens might otherwise be, you know, enjoying themselves, a thousand studious adolescents find themselves sitting portions of a practice selective-school exam. You can imagine their heads bent diligently over their desks, a balmy breeze wafting in every so often from the outside.

This scene, written up in *The Sydney Morning Herald*, is rather coy about the ethnic make-up of the majority of test-takers. But given that the story is fundamentally about tuition, a sector with at least 75% Asian clientele, take a guess what background might heavily feature in the crowd?

These opening illustrations aren't meant to (further) stigmatise the Asian, overachieving student – often a figure of pity, if you're feeling indulgent, or irritation, if they're topping English as well as Maths. I'm telling you about Tina Huang and the academic strivers at Olympic Park because, as a Chinese high achiever myself talking about achievement addiction, I'm tapping into one of the most controversial issues in education in this country: the dominance of Asian students in public selective schools. So we may as well deal with that elephant – or tiger mother and her dragon child – in the room.

Yes, I might be leveraging unhelpful stereotypes here – of the Asian straight-A student – that I personally have felt the pressure of and want to challenge. Yes, I'm taking the risk of perpetuating the myth of the 'model minority' that assumes that all Asians are studious, self-reliant, and hard-working, when Asians are just as diverse as any other group. And yes, thank God I'm Chinese, or I'd be crazy to rush in where the white woke fear to tread.

Yes, yes, and yes.

But I must also confess that I can't help but marvel at Asian high achievers. They – we – are people of grit who work extremely hard to reach their goals. As such, they merit our attention because they – and their highly motivated parents – are the ideal citizens of the meritocracy, or the equal opportunity system where the hardest workers rise to the top.

To make my case, I give you the pushiest parent of them all.

An ambush of tigers

'My goal as a parent is to prepare you for the future – not to make you like me.'

The Tiger Mom is nothing if not blunt, as you'll find if you ever read Amy Chua's *Battle Hymn of the Tiger Mother* (2011). Chua's obsession with her daughters' accomplishments and her shameless belief in the superiority of Chinese parenting shocked Western audiences, making her parenting memoir an instant bestseller and the subject of countless think pieces tiptoeing around the racially loaded topic.

Among Chua's many notorieties: forcing hours of daily musical practice on her kids so they could audition for Julliard or play Carnegie Hall – even if one of her girls had been known to gnaw on the piano as a stressed-out six-year-old. Then there was the non-option of refusing optional schoolwork. As Chua recalled berating Lulu, her youngest daughter: 'You went to *recess* instead of doing *extra credit*?'

These days, that's not that outrageous. Apparently, there's an elite primary school in New York City that sets students a daily problem that requires solving by the final bell – without any class time dedicated to it. The reason is that if these kids are to become tomorrow's wolves of Wall Street, they need to practice wringing productivity out of every spare moment. I mean, who needs to run around during lunch time, anyway?

It's as though Amy Chua's extreme parenting freaked everyone out – and then they took notes.

Since the controversy over Chua's book, it's become apparent that it's a bit rich to single out her single-mindedness about achievement. Plenty of others, it turns out, are exactly the same.

For instance, everyone knows a 'white tiger parent' obsessed with their kids' sporting success. The white-tiger parent is nothing if not committed – no sweat getting Matty or Charlotte poolside by 6am for laps. But their 'coaching' and 'refereeing' from the sidelines of weekend sporting comps tends to ruin everyone's fun. This kind of behaviour means that today, it's not uncommon to see signs reminding parents to 'keep sport fun', to remember 'referees are human too.' After all, 'this is NOT the A-League or the World Cup.'

As well as the white-tiger parent, there's also the tiger coach. In 2021, Gymnastics Australia was rocked by revelations of abusive treatment of young gymnasts. The Human Rights Commission report called out authoritarian coaching styles, a culture of fear, bullying, and harassment, as well as a gruelling 'win at all costs' mentality that marked the effort to turn young gymnasts into Olympians.

Particularly revealing is a letter from Peggy Liddick, the national women's coach, to Sarah Lauren, a teenage gymnast who quit after winning two gold medals at the Manchester Commonwealth Games. 'You say you do not want to work hard anymore. Well, Sarah, you have no idea what *real hard work is*', Liddell wrote in a masterclass of passive aggression. 'If you think that you have worked hard, at just 15 years old and only one National Team, you are very much mistaken.'

Liddick also channelled her inner tiger parent when she dismissed Commonwealth gold compared to the Olympics ('the top of the mountain'), and sniffed that 'no degree or academic record can replace having that "Olympian" on your résumé.'

After all the hand-wringing over Chua's extreme parenting, it turns out that she's not that unusual after all. Tiger coaches and white-tiger parents are just as obsessed about success – and not above behaviour that makes the original Tiger Mom almost seem tame.

Obviously, the fact that tigers happen to come in all stripes doesn't make tiger-rearing styles okay. But it should check the temptation to single out Asian tiger parents for particular criticism.

Everyone is a concerted cultivator

Minus the abuse, the tiger approach is an extreme version of 'concerted cultivation': a parenting strategy designed to futureproof children in a competitive schooling and jobs environment. This is not just helicopter parenting that gets everyone's eyes rolling. This is the serious business of raising a future worker/human who can thrive in an insecure job market.

Concerted cultivation describes the way parents' lives (let's be real: probably the lives of mums) revolve around enriching, organised activities for the kids – like annual museum memberships, planned play dates, sport camps, art classes. And, just to clarify, we're now talking ordinary kids – not budding Olympians who expect to dedicate exceptional levels of time and commitment to their sport.

With both my kids now in school, I'm learning a lot about what concerted cultivation looks like in my neighbourhood. Take, for example, the average party for a seven-year-old today. Picnic in the park? Hide-and-seek in the backyard? So passé. What about a guided session of ninja gym, trampolining, karate, or bouldering? Today, it's not unusual for the whole class at school to get invited to *another* class outside of it to celebrate a birthday. Kids get directly instructed what to do when, food arrives right on time, and parents go home extra satisfied because the kids have had fun *and* been productive simultaneously.

If you detect a cynical tone here, I need to come clean: I throw this kind of party myself. It's far easier than hosting a birthday party at my place that I'll have to clean up later – that's the last thing an overscheduled, exhausted parent needs. So if you can afford to outsource the whole affair, I say go for it.

But it's worth noting one particular side effect of concerted cultivation. Apparently, it grooms kids for bougie, professional life: high on structure, planning, schedule-keeping, and reaching goals. You could argue that in socialising kids to be productive, even in their leisure time, concerted cultivation sets up kids to be endlessly busy. Exhausted, even. Like their bougie parents.

How different is this, really, from the life of your average Asian high-achieving student?

Though the context and the details may differ, surely the way we middle-class parents overschedule our children with enriching activities is on the *same spectrum* as the Asian migrant parent who throws money at tuition to help their kid ace the selective-schools exam. Perhaps the Asian tiger parent, in other words, is just a more hardcore version of the average concerted cultivator.

And one whose tiger parenting is driven by no

small measure of economic anxiety. As University of Technology Sydney academic Christina Ho explores in *Aspiration and Anxiety: Asian Migrants and Australian Schooling*, fears of job discrimination and a lack of social connections means that plenty of Asian migrant parents seek impeccable educational credentials for their children.

Ho rejects the tiger-parenting approach for the way it instrumentalises learning. But she also questions resentment against Asian parents while the government's preference for skilled migrants escapes scrutiny. After all, ambitious, high-achieving migrant professionals aren't likely to relax their interest in achievement and education when it comes to their kids. It's unfair to blame Asian migrants, Ho argues, for working within the rules of a game set up by others.

As Ho sees it, the migrant is left poised between aspiration and anxiety: a desire to succeed in a new country, accompanied by angst over their prospects. If that was your situation, what would you do?

Asian migrant kids resort to working like … well, Asians when it comes to their qualifications. Which is probably why a Lowy Institute survey of Chinese-Australians found that almost half (46%) had a bachelor's degree or higher, compared to a quarter (26%) of the Australian population at large.

Indeed, in some Asian-Australian migrant households, the life of the house revolves around children's homework routines. In solidarity with the intense workload shouldered by their kids, parents might even go so far as to ban TV for everyone, says Ho. As might you, if people with surnames like yours had to submit 68% more applications to get an interview, as studies have found.

In *Battle Hymn of the Tiger Mother*, Amy Chua's daughter Lulu declared, 'I don't really have time for anything fun because I'm Chinese.' Lulu may be a child of privilege, but what she says might also go for the average migrant kid. No fun just might be the price you pay when your tiger parents believe your future success is at stake.

Everyone is kind of Asian now

Perhaps strangely, this furious work ethic also makes Asians an example and/or cautionary tale to all of us in a culture obsessed with hard-won success. After all, Asians aren't the only ones stuck pounding the achievement treadmill.

That's because our achievement-addicted culture runs in tandem with a market economy. One that prizes competition, rewards individual initiative, and puts a price on everything – even people. We may not be for sale, strictly speaking, but we're treated as commodities or as bearers of human capital. Everyone gets assigned a market value depending on our abilities, experience, and intelligence. From this perspective, the human is basically a bundle of achievements, or a walking, talking résumé.

Or an ATAR on legs, if you're at school – the

Australian equivalent of SATs in the United States, or A Levels in the United Kingdom. In which case, spare a thought for the young people who don't rate highly according to scholastic measures of achievement. Like Eden Wallis, whose learning difficulties made it hard for her to sit her final school exams:

> There's a lot that I do know, it's just that I can't put it on paper. I need to express myself in other ways. Unfortunately, that's just how the education system is ... It's sad that that's the only way that people are measured against, their [academic] intelligence. I feel it now when people ask me what I got, and I don't tell anyone. I don't want this number to define who I am.

Eden resists being reduced to a number, and no wonder: it's dehumanising. But dominant market values encourage us to see ourselves in such terms – and to work extremely hard to maintain our worth.

The work of getting and maintaining high human capital means we get into survival-of-the-fittest mode, doing what we can to remain as competitive as possible. Long after the ATAR, we're still vying with each other for the same rewards, jobs, and status.

Things like hobbies become hard to sustain, because whatever is pursued for fun and enjoyment just takes time away from what we should be doing instead: more work. We can feel a needling guilt when we're not working – even on days off. These are signs that we've internalised the non-stop work mentality of 'millennial burnout', according to Anne

Helen Petersen, the prophet and chronicler of that contemporary condition. No matter the exhaustion, you just have to keep going. Life hacks that solve multiple problems simultaneously seem a godsend: grabbing a coffee with a friend and going on a brisk walk together means both of us can strike exercise and socialising off our never-ending To Do lists.

You might start to feel as though life is a series of exams you need to ace, or the endless pursuit of experiences and qualifications that will look good on a résumé. If this sounds familiar, you just might be an 'excellent sheep', as William Deresiewicz, a former Yale professor, put it. Deresiewicz meant, more specifically, young American students pursuing an elite, Ivy League education: people he praised as talented, driven, and achievement-oriented – who also happened to be morally incurious about life beyond their academic track record. But his designation of 'excellent sheep' fits many of us – with our yen for optimisation and inability to chillax – all too well.

And there's no shortage of instruments inviting us to rate and rank ourselves against each other: pay scales, the desirability (or not) of the postcodes we inhabit, the number of followers we have on social media, what accolades we can boast of, the rites of polite small talk (' … and what do you do for a living?'), where we went to school. In fact, Bri Lee notes in *Who Gets to Be Smart: Privilege, Power and Knowledge* that these kinds of questions make for standard small talk in status-obsessed Sydney.

Whatever your answers to these queries, they become not-so-subtle indicators of value that ascribe greater human capital to, say, a CEO as opposed to a pizza delivery driver, or a chief scientist versus a childcare worker. Value that's reflected in our pay packets, and/or in social recognition of our contributions.

If a number is going to be affixed to your name, and that number is indexed to monetary rewards, the esteem of others, and your self-satisfaction, then it makes sense to work, work, and work to best position yourself for your future success.

This means that, in the end, it's not only the actual Asians who are toiling away to make it in the world. We all are. As far as I'm concerned, that makes everyone an honorary Asian.

You are *my* people, after all.

Re:CONSIDERING

2. SUFFER

Ever tried barre? Not pronouncing it, mind you, as Australian Prime Minister Scott Morrison struggled to when announcing restrictions on gyms because of the pandemic. But – actually – enduring it?

Fusing ballet and pilates, barre is like that *Jurassic World* dinosaur that's part-velociraptor, part-T-Rex. Basically, take the deadliest parts of each to make a more lethal killing machine. Or, in this case, a workout regime that promises the lean look of the ballet dancer, since they have the kind of body that many women would kill for – themselves, as it turns out. More pain, more gain – you know how it goes.

The worst part of barre is, honestly, *all of it*. The class is one wave of agony after another as you make incremental movements – called isometric exercises – in time to a frantic beat. The physiology of what's happening is impenetrable to me but it *burns*.

In one class, I hovered in a seated position while holding on to the barre, heels lifted as I bobbed up and down an inch with control. The work of that minute movement while staying in place was gruelling. 'Smile, ladies!' the instructor called gaily – because even if it's torturous work, you're supposed to *like it*.

For essayist Jia Tolentino, barre's emphasis on

ceaseless, strenuous work does more than dangle before you the promise of a ballerina body:

> The endurance that barre builds is possibly more psychological than physical. What it's really good at is getting you in shape for a hyper-accelerated capitalist life … As a form of exercise, barre is ideal for an era in which everyone has to work constantly – you can be back at the office in five minutes, no shower necessary …

Tolentino has a point – even if she's dead wrong about *not* needing a shower afterwards. The hard work of barre seamlessly blends in with every other part of life where you're already working. In an achievement-addicted culture, a fit body not only looks good but also broadcasts your capacity for hard and constant work. Physical fitness, in other words, requires the same traits that both honorary and actual Asians need to flourish within an exhausting meritocracy: discipline, endurance, self-control, and responsibility.

Maybe being an achievement addict isn't exactly like signing up for an excruciating exercise class. But the arduous work required to develop your human capital – and then maintain it for the rest of your life – comes close.

It's important to mention, however, that life as an achievement addict is not all pain. There's also a sick delight in being so hardcore. Getting fit may involve hard work and suffering, but the pay-off is considerable: a 'good' body, and the proud realisation that you have effected your own transformation. Similarly, achievement addiction may be harmful to yourself and others, but the pleasure of success offers pretty intense highs.

In the previous chapter, we established that an achievement-addicted culture demands such a stringent work ethic that it makes honorary Asians of us all. Now, we train our gaze on the way work, suffering, and pleasure all converge for the achievement addict. We also explore what we have invested spiritually in our addictions and what we get out of them.

Pleasure-pain projects

Barre is a classic example of what I call a *pleasure-pain project*. Granted, a label like that makes it sound particularly perverse. But we're engaged in pleasure-pain projects all the time: activities that entwine the pain of hard work with the pleasure of being so productive – and all for a desired goal. Here are three.

Fitbit addiction

If you wear a Fitbit long enough, you'll eventually ask yourself a question to which you intuitively know the answer: if a run isn't tracked, did it really happen? (No.) In short, you become rather obsessed with your metrics.

You might also chafe at only hitting that conventional target of 10,000 steps a day. That's for mere mortals. One Pauline Craven-Lee told *The Daily*

Mail that if she doesn't reach her daily goal – 30,000 steps – she'll step out in all kinds of weather until the numbers are right, or risk feeling anxious and having trouble sleeping at night.

On Pauline's best day, she hit 68,000 steps. This meant that, 'from 6.30am, when I took my dogs out for a walk, until 10.30pm, I exercised non-stop, including two gym classes and a long run on the treadmill. But although I was elated, I really paid for it the next day with sore feet and aching hips.'

Feeling great and awful at the same time – welcome to the pleasure-pain of Fitbit addiction. One where positive results and rewards motivate you to keep going, and to keep edging up your daily target – even if your body protests. Even if you can't quite remember what you're doing it *for*.

It's not that you're addicted to walking, per se. Perhaps what traps you in that endless loop of work, suffering, and pleasure is the feeling that *you can change* if only you muster the requisite willpower and determination. That ultimately, you can be in charge of your life, if only you are prepared to suffer for it. This fantasy of control is hard to resist – even if, in this case, the trade-off is becoming a literal walking machine.

#mumlife optimised

Becoming a mother is as incredible as it is incredibly confronting. You experience physical changes – some of which can only be called *body horror*. You used to eat, and now another human feeds on you. Then there's the sweeping and often permanent adjustments to your (in no particular order) life, timetable, peace of mind, and level of acceptable mess. Becoming a mum can bring you to the absolute end of yourself.

So, of course, some mums on social-media just have to make motherhood look *amazing*. At one extreme end, you've got mum influencers showing off their buttery, stretch mark-free skin and compact baby bumps. Or posts of the whole family clad in matchy-matchy pastel. That's if mum is actually wearing anything, rather than posing naked (tastefully) on her resort-worthy balcony because 'all of your maternity clothing is in storage and nothing is quite fitting anymore 🙈'.

This fantasy of motherhood is so ridiculous and entertaining that I find it hard to begrudge its existence. At least we know it's not real. But let's be honest: the rest of us achievement-addicted mums are doing our own scaled-down version of optimised #mumlife and treating motherhood as a competitive sport.

It may not be through perfect holiday snaps but, for example, the way we parent in public. Like the way we sweetly and persistently reason with the kids to stop kicking the chair in front of them, rather than the blunt 'cut it out' we would've issued had we not been under the gaze of other mums. Or the way we pack uber-healthy, environmentally conscious school lunches, with nary a Tiny Teddy packet in sight. Judging by the veggie sticks that populate the lunchboxes of social media, some parents are raising rabbit-children who know not the evils of processed food.

As anyone with more than a passing knowledge of parenthood would know, motherhood is infrequently blissful, orderly, nutritionally balanced, or perfectly lit. And any woman who wants to set herself the challenge of making it seem as such is clearly into pleasure-pain. Caring for kids is difficult enough without also being spotlessly made-up, maintaining your figure, having your home look photo shoot-ready, and taking endless selfies of all of the above.

But the pay-off of all that effort, I suppose, is emerging triumphant from the battlefield of the only mummy war worth winning: the one that declares you the best (and the fairest, shh) mum of them all.

Our property obsession

In Australia, the ultimate pleasure-pain project can be summed up in one word: property.

The Australian dream of owning your own home may seem out of reach for young people today, given skyrocketing property prices and stagnant wages growth. But you can still own your own home. You just have to work hard enough.

That's the gist, anyway, of what 35-year-old millionaire and real-estate magnate Tim Gurner told *60 Minutes* a few years ago: 'When I had my first business when I was 19, I was in the gym at 6am in the morning, and I finished at 10.30 at night, and I did it seven days a week, and I did it until I could afford my first home,' he told the program. 'There was no discussions around, could I go out for breakfast, could I go out for dinner. I just worked.'

And judging by that answer, Gurner felt proud of all his disciplined labor. But not only could young people work on their work ethic, however. They could also be more thrifty, he said. When asked if young people might never own a home, Gurner responded, 'Absolutely, when you're spending \$40 a day on smashed avocados and coffees and not working. Of course.'

Ahh, the return of the smashed avocado: the bane of the existence of all aspiring homeowners. Since Bernard Salt's satirical column in *The Australian* mocking expensive brunch items that could otherwise be put towards a home deposit, fears have abounded that young people are spoiled brats with lavish tastes. Even if the tongue-in-cheek Avocado Index of housing affordability found that based on average house prices in Sydney in 2016 (at just over AUD\$1,000,000), people would need to forsake 46,509 avocado toasts every day for 127 years to pay for a house.

But let's entertain, for the moment, Gurner's claim: that we lazy renters whining about house prices could learn a thing or two about forgoing immediate pleasures for a long-term payoff. We're the cicadas of that Aesop fable who spend careless summers at play while industrious ant homeowners store up food for the winter.

If you remember that story, once the cicada comes begging for food at wintertime, the ant tells it to get lost. The ant has not only worked hard; it has also sacrificed much in order to reach its goal. What, pray tell, has the cicada done to earn access to the ant's stash? Absolutely nothing. The cicada has not, in other words, proved worthy of the pleasure-pain pay-off.

Suffering for success, the fable implies, carries moral weight and increases your deservingness. Hence, the moral of that story goes: 'work today to eat tomorrow.' For my housing-stressed generation, the lesson might be: forgo avo today to avo home tomorrow.

Work as salvation

Each of these pleasure-pain projects reveals just what we're prepared to suffer in service of a larger goal. If we want something badly enough, the thinking goes, we'll make sacrifices to get it. Our national property obsession shows that even deprivation is appealing if it shows how worthy we are of success.

But for William Deresiewicz, the professor who popularised the 'excellent sheep' term, the pleasure of being exceptional can hollow you out from within. 'I've experienced the pleasure of succeeding, the pleasure of being lauded,' he told me in an interview. 'But it reminds me of something that I've heard: anorexic girls, especially the pro-anas and pro-mias will say: "nothing tastes as good as being thin feels."'

Delving into the psychology of that thinking,

Deresiewicz speculates: 'I mean, you feel like you've won. You feel like you're pretty, but actually you feel horrible because you're starving. And that's my analogy for the feeling of being at the top. Nothing feels as good as the taste of victory, but I don't think it's nourishing.'

That's the pleasure-pain predicament right there: we can't quit the thing that requires our suffering.

These pleasure-pain stories are also examples of what journalist Ben Tarnoff calls 'conspicuous production' or 'the public display of productivity'. It's the work equivalent of 'conspicuous consumption' – only instead of signalling your bank balance through what you buy, you instead flaunt your immense industry. For Tarnoff, conspicuous production manifests as an extreme work ethic more commonly seen among Silicon Valley CEOs – like Jack Dorsey, CEO of Twitter and Square.

Each day, Dorsey does two hours of gruelling meditation, walks eight kilometres to work a few times a week (before COVID-19, anyway), and eats one meal per weekday before fasting all weekend. Oh, and he has ice baths first thing in the morning – his version, it seems, of a pep talk: 'I feel like if I can will myself to do that thing that seems so small but hurts so much, I can do nearly anything.'

Dorsey's daily habits are next level compared with the more ordinary pleasure-pain projects chronicled above. But these stories all share a common core. They revel in their distinct versions of achievement addiction. These stories tap into the thrill of being exceptional and our desire to prove ourselves worthy of any challenge before us. They allow us the fantasy of feeling powerful, being in control, and enjoying the pride – glory, even – of all our hard work paying off. In stories like these, we get to be the heroes who bend the world to our will through sheer effort.

Philosopher Andrew Taggart detects a spiritual understory to all this striving – one that applies to all of us. For Taggart, Dorsey is a 'secular monk'. Monk, because Dorsey is furiously devoted to ascetic self-control – witness the deprivation of his daily routine. Secular, because secular monks believe in neither God nor transcendence. For secular monks, this world is all there is, and so those who would flourish need to optimise themselves for peak performance.

Secular monks 'commit to work – to working on themselves and on the world – as the key to salvation', Taggart observes. Self-work, in other words, forms the horizon of their ultimate hopes. Help isn't coming from anywhere else, so the individual must accept responsibility for the success (or otherwise) of their life.

If you fail to thrive, this can be a punishing vision. But if you flourish, your self-work and hard-won success can be a source of immense pride. The world may be a lonely husk emptied of ultimate meaning. But by the strength of your will, you have prevailed and made something of yourself.

In which case, you'd be the closest thing to god

in a godless universe. This is the existential secret of achievement addiction: you want to earn your own salvation. You want to be your own god, and the basis of all meaning.

But there's a risk to basing your meaning – and your identity – on your exceptionality.

A lonely girl

Jessie Tu's celebrated novel, *A Lonely Girl is a Dangerous Thing*, tells the story of Jena Lin, a former violin prodigy, trying to revive her career after a public breakdown at 15 years old.

Seven years later, Jena fills the void left by fame through sex. 'In the absence of acclaim for my musicianship, getting a boy into bed was as fulfilling and joyful as any other accomplishment', she says. Jena gets that she has swapped one arena of achievement for another.

But there's more going on. At times, Jena alludes to 'a hole in me that was ultimately unfillable.' There's a lot going on in this lack. It describes, alternately, the depths of Jena's untapped talent, her insatiable hunger for recognition of her unique gifts, and her all-consuming need to play the violin.

We get a sense of that need through Tu's ecstatic descriptions of Jena's violin-playing. These passages show us both the transcendence Jena experiences, and yet also the mental and bodily agony of performing. While mid-piece during an audition,

Jena is pricked by panic that she won't be able to keep going, yet she manages to finish triumphantly. Her normally hard calluses burst, however, 'leaving damp layers of skin peeling off, half attached. It feels like I've plunged my fingertips into a bowl of razor blades.'

I bet Jack Dorsey knows what that kind of euphoria feels like. Jena is no secular monk, but she has plenty in common with the CEO. The physical strain of their obsessive routines. The mental tautness. The undeniable highs. I wonder if these three states feel, for both Dorsey and Jena, indistinguishable from each other. Dorsey may be a tech titan, and Jena a fictional violin prodigy, but both are achievement addicts who have made a career in pleasure-pain. Even if they have to suffer for their art, the pain itself is part of the ecstasy of achievement.

True, there's plenty of pleasure on offer: the gratification of being a true believer who is furiously committed to the cause. Perhaps the praise of others is too hard to give up. Or the rewards: money, status, fame. But what might be really addictive, I'd wager, is the sick thrill of how much you can accomplish even when you're beaten down and so exhausted you can barely do anything else.

But what *A Lonely Girl* reveals is how deep the requisite suffering works its way into the soul. So much of Jena is wrapped up in her gifts (and the burden of them) that she fears that she is nobody without them: 'I'd stare at myself in the mirror in the bathroom and wonder if one day I'd look and there would be no one staring back at me.'

Perhaps this is yet another way to understand Jena's lack. The desire to be someone is overwhelming, even for someone as obviously talented as her. And yet the very thing that she suffers for, and that makes her special, also seems incredibly dissatisfying. It doesn't guarantee her identity, which leaves Jena permanently stuck in the groove of pleasure-pain. She's compelled to reach greater and more intense highs, but without any promise of actual deliverance.

This is the plight of the achievement addict. Like Jena, they're a lonely girl in a lonely world. With a void that nothing seems able to fill.

3. SMUG

Call me a rotten class traitor, but I don't care. I can't stand *The West Wing*.

The celebrated political drama series may have ended in 2006, but the show remains a touchstone for left-leaning ideals today. Indeed, so deep is the liberal attachment to the fictional Democratic administration of President Josiah Bartlet that *The West Wing* was a prime candidate for comfort watching in the era of President Donald Trump. 'When I feel the need for comfort from the circus in the White House, I watch the pilot', one superfan named Terry Callanan told the *New York Times* in 2019. 'Seriously, almost every night before I go to sleep.'

Since there's a different occupant in the White House these days, perhaps Callanan is living the dream, and not just seeking refuge in one. But what if you're more politically conservative? Or you don't have the polish or the impressive résumés of the political staffers on screen? Sure, you have plenty of your own comfort viewing. But if you don't share *The West Wing's* politics, then its overt fantasising about clever and noble liberals running the country is both arrogant and insulting. Seen from that perspective, the show comes off as rather smug.

And smug, it turns out, is the particular temptation of the achievement addict. The fact is that achievement addiction makes more than one groove in the soul. If, as we saw in the last chapter, we rely on our achievements to secure our identity, then this chapter will show how we are tempted to relate to others on the basis of our achievements.

Smugness, of course, is the resting state of the self-satisfied, which always relies on others being worse off in comparison. It's why smug behaviour triggers such angry outbursts from those who feel diminished as a result. *You think you're better than me.* No other six words so grimly sweat resentment.

Smugness and sweaty resentment also happen to describe the toxic dynamic between those who thrive in a meritocracy and those who don't. This was the insight of Michael Young, a British sociologist, who originally coined the term 'meritocracy' in *The Rise of the Meritocracy, 1870–2033* (1958). Young's book was a dystopian satire describing his dire predictions for a world where success and recognition tracked an individual's hard work and talent – the very world we have worked so hard to create in the decades since.

Because today, of course, we're big believers in the meritocratic ideal. Since a meritocracy levels the playing field, we think it's a more equal, democratic, and just system. No one's rank, birth, or wealth should guarantee them a head start in life, we believe. We're fully on board with the meritocratic mentality: that *hard work + perseverance = success you have rightly earned.*

But Young warned that a meritocratic mentality would prove double-edged. If hard work was the arbiter of success, he argued, society would be divided between meritocracy's 'winners' – the deserving haves – and 'losers' – the undeserving have-nots. The 'losers' would end up feeling as though they hadn't tried hard enough, and they would blame themselves for their failures. The 'winners', on the other hand, would feel like they'd rightly earned their success and position in life – and look down on everyone else.

They would fall prey to what American political philosopher Michael J. Sandel calls 'meritocratic hubris', or the tendency to 'inhale too deeply of their success.'

I can't help but feel as though *The West Wing* indulges meritocratic winners with a big fat whiff.

It stinks.

A modern fairytale

The West Wing lost me in its pilot episode when White House Chief of Staff Leo McGarry rang *The New York Times* to let them know about a mistake in its daily crossword. Judging by McGarry's befuddled reaction, he must have received a stroppy reply from the person on the other end of the line.

It's a brief moment, but one that tells you a lot about McGarry and the show's intended audience: problem solvers who are good with words, detail oriented, and so permanently *on* that, work or play, they're always performing some variation of the same word-centred, detail-driven exercise.

The show, it turns out, tested well with university-educated, *New York Times*-reading types, and went on to find a devoted fan base among political staffers, policy wonks, and journos. *The West Wing* succeeded, then, in courting viewers who were like the people it portrayed: white-collar professionals, the managerial class, and members of the political establishment. In other words, the elite – which I mean not as an insult, but in the neutral sense to describe the well-educated.

A poor kid from a broken home, fostered out repeatedly, and with military service on his résumé, Rob Henderson knew immediately that he was not *The West Wing*'s intended audience. But the show, he says, gave him 'an aspirational roadmap for upward mobility.'

His military-assigned Ivy League tutors were obsessed with *The West Wing*, seeing future versions of themselves on screen. So Rob studied them studying the show, and gradually picked up meritocratic values and attitudes – like the importance of a good education.

TV, in other words, taught Rob how to escape his class: through a university degree. Fairy godmother may have sent Cinderella to the ball, but TV propelled Rob into the doctoral program at the University of Cambridge. A modern fairytale – of sorts.

But what TV really taught Rob was credentialism: the belief that a four-year university degree was the baseline for success. Which means that if you lack those kinds of qualifications, you bear a social cost.

In fact, surveys from the United Kingdom, the United States, the Netherlands, and Belgium have suggested that the university-educated dislike the poorly educated *the most* out of other discriminated-against groups like Muslims, African-Americans, the working class, the obese, and the blind. The highly educated respondents, moreover, weren't exactly embarrassed to admit to their bias.

Perhaps, the survey's authors reasoned, the respondents believed that the disadvantage experienced by those other minorities was beyond anyone's control. Yet education, the thinking went, was surely within someone's grasp – if they wanted it badly enough. The respondents' meritocratic mentality, in other words, regarded the failure to be educated as an individual responsibility, and so felt their harsh judgement was deserved.

Education, we tend to think, is supposed to make you more enlightened and tolerant. But being educated is no guarantee that you won't also be prejudiced – which, no doubt, comes as a shock to … elites.

Remember *Hoarders* – that TV show that helps North Americans cull the possessions they're drowning in? You don't exactly picture a degree from Harvard askew on the wall behind that stack of yellowing newspapers. And yet credentialism outs educated elites as *shocking* hoarders – not of shoe polish or empty coffee pods, but intangibles like honour and respect.

That's because university degrees do more than set you up for life (that's the pitch, anyway). They're also the ticket to social esteem. If credentials are the prerequisite for that kind of recognition, what's it like to be *un*credentialled?

'Deplorables'

We don't exactly have to guess. Populist protests in the United Kingdom with the Brexit vote and in the United States with the election of Donald Trump to the presidency have been fueled by what Michael Sandel calls a 'politics of humiliation'.

This is the flipside of meritocratic hubris. Except where hubris involves a sense of pride and self-congratulation, a politics of humiliation concerns the way that meritocracy's losers are harshly judged

– whether by themselves or others – for their lack of success.

Trump appealed powerfully to that grievance in his presidential campaign and beyond. Of those who voted for him, he won two-thirds of votes among people without a university degree, while over 70 percent of voters with advanced degrees threw their support behind the Democratic presidential nominee Hillary Clinton. So the 2016 election split the country into two factions: the credentialled and the uncredentialled.

Trump cast himself as the champion of the latter by channelling the anger and economic anxiety of working people, for whom stagnant wages, jobs moving offshore, and insecure work had eroded self-respect, social standing, and living standards. As president, his inaugural address railed against the way 'the wealth of our middle class has been ripped from their homes and then redistributed across the entire world.' He vowed that the 'forgotten men and women of our country will be forgotten no longer.' Not quite the uplifting rhetoric we've come to expect from the leader of the most powerful nation in the world.

This suggests that Trump's promise to 'make America great again' had to do with restoring something vital – something keenly human – that had been unfairly stripped away. Not merely status, income, future prospects, or even a reliably middle-class existence – but dignity.

In an article that went viral after the 2016 US presidential election, Joan C. Williams explained why working people backed the billionaire: not just because of his promise to revive the fortunes of blue-collar masculinity, but also his intolerance for political correctness, and the fact that he wasn't a professional politician. Working people, Williams said, loathe professionals, seeing them as blowhards who know nothing but tell everyone else how to do their job. And Hillary Clinton seemed the consummate professional. It didn't help, either, that she wrote off Trump's supporters as a 'basket of deplorables'.

Which brings us back to *The West Wing*.

Essayist Luke Savage has observed that the show refrains from depicting politics as a terrain of competing values and interests. Instead it's more interested, he says, in showcasing opportunities for the smart to smugly fend off the dumb.

Even Clinton's 'deplorables' comment, Savage says, seems right at home with a rhetorical strategy proposed by Toby Ziegler. In the episode 'Hartsfield's Landing' from Season 3, President Bartlet wonders whether his being the 'smartest kid in the class' works against his re-election chances. Should he be more 'folksy' and 'plain spoken' with voters instead? Ziegler dismisses such talk: 'Make this election about smart, and not. Make it about engaged, and not. Qualified, and not. Make it about a heavyweight. You're a heavyweight.' In other words, emphasise how good and smart you are, and the impossibility of your opponents ever measuring up.

There's nothing wrong with being smart, by the way. Clever people are often excellent company. And if I get a say in who should run the country, I'll choose intelligent and competent leaders over inexperienced cranks every time. But as I've learned from extensive personal experience, an occupational hazard of considering yourself smart is having a big head about it.

The world according to Ravenclaw

Maybe what irks me most about *The West Wing* is the way it remakes the world in the image of the meritocratic elite. And sure, every interest group wants the world to better reflect their priorities and concerns. But I bet that die-hard fans of the show are also the kind of people who, in principle at least, want the interests of all people represented, rather than those of one narrow class.

That class prizes meritocratic values: being clever, working hard, acquiring credentials, and rising through the ranks. Nothing wrong with that value set, in and of itself. But the problem is when these traits monopolise the way we measure success and become the criteria for bestowing recognition on others. In contrast, other praiseworthy things – like honesty, doing your duty, being a 'good' person – just don't seem to matter as much.

The West Wing version of reality is kind of like, to cite another beloved cultural text, the world according to Ravenclaw. While Gryffindor and Slytherin duked it out in *Harry Potter*, our world seems more split between the other two Hogwarts houses: Ravenclaw and Hufflepuff.

That's because Ravenclaw traits – cleverness, competitiveness, and the tendency to be arch about their undeniable gifts – naturally signify it as the home of the meritocratic elite. In contrast, Hufflepuff characteristics – being loyal, kind, and hard-working – seem lame consolation for not being all that bright. As Hagrid once said, 'Everyone says Hufflepuff are a lot o' duffers.'

Maybe they are, and maybe they aren't. It just doesn't seem to matter so much in the world of *Harry Potter*. Our achievement-addicted world, however, seems more hung up on being clever and credentialled.

Journalist David Goodhart, for instance, aptly describes the world ruled by the interests of Ravenclaw. It's one where 'one form of human aptitude – cognitive-analytical ability, the talent that helps people to pass exams and then handle information efficiently in their professional lives – has become the *gold standard of human esteem.'*

As a result, the dominance of knowledge workers in an information economy – what Goodhart broadly labels Head work – devalues the pay and status of manual labour and care work. In his terms, Head gets all the glory, while the contributions of Heart and Hand are undervalued.

If Goodhart was describing a human body, it would be rather lopsided and lack integrity – which we'll come back to in Chapter 4. But such imbalance is also bad for the body politic. Such an inequality of esteem can have profound impacts on people. It can diminish people's standing in the eyes of others, and also in their own. It can cause them to lose hope for themselves and their children. And it can also cost lives.

In fact, in the United States over the past decade, life expectancy has declined for White Americans as 'deaths of despair' have ravaged the country: deaths from suicide, drug overdoses, and alcohol abuse. Declining job prospects and diminished self-respect explain this tragic picture, say the Princeton economists who coined the term.

Additionally, white middle-aged men and women without a four-year university degree are particularly vulnerable to dying from self-harm. 'A four-year degree has become *the* key marker of social status, as if there were a requirement for nongraduates to wear a circular scarlet badge bearing the letters *BA* crossed through by a diagonal line', write Anne Case and Angus Deaton of the social cost borne by the uncredentialled. As Daniel Markovits has vividly described, such deaths of despair 'somatise the insult' of economic exclusion. Real bodies, in other words, bear the brunt of a system that regards them as worthless.

It's not about everyone getting a trophy

What we've really been tracking in this chapter is the dissolution of common bonds with each other. It's hard to remember that we're all part of the same human team when some players (so to speak) get a louder roar from the crowd than others. Currently, our achievement-obsessed culture tends to single out the clever and the credentialled for praise and high pay, which makes it harder for those of us with different abilities and experience to be recognised.

Which, by the way, is not a sentimental argument for everyone to get a trophy, or to deny people proper recognition for their achievements. It makes sense to reward talent and effort, and to seek the best, most qualified candidates to fulfil the most demanding roles. But when one measure of human value is so prevalent, it's easy to forget that there is no single scale of human worth. For instance, Ravenclaw may emphasise intelligence, but Gryffindor, Hufflepuff, and Slytherin highlight, respectively, bravery, loyalty, and, er, megalomaniacal ambition as significant human traits.

And as I've also explored through moaning about *The West Wing*, smart people might also be particularly prone to being smug people. Or unwise people. Or unkind people. It's ironic that the cleverest people among us can still be blindsided by their own prejudices. Especially since they also happen to be the kind of people who pride themselves on their ability to see the bigger picture.

Michael Young, meritocracy's original critic, feared that the world of equal opportunity would merely swap one class system for another. That aristocracy, or rule by the rich, would be replaced by meritocracy that would establish its own privileged caste of the clever.

If we aren't to be smug or resentful with each other on the basis of our achievements – or on our lack of them – then we need to find a better way that we can belong with each other.

4. STORY TIME

'The universe is made of stories, not of atoms', the poet Muriel Rukeyser famously observed.

Atoms may be the basic unit of all existence, but our dependence on story for meaning and significance is just as foundational. We rely on narrative to make sense of the world and our place within it, and to give us direction and clarity: what happy ending we should aim our lives at, and what we should do in order to get it. In doing so, stories don't simply illuminate who we are right now but, crucially, who we might become.

So it matters greatly what stories you live by.

Rob Henderson, who we met in the last chapter, recognises how influential *The West Wing* was on him: it taught him how to escape his class. He's left musing, however, whether TV taught him what to want in the first place. In other words, whether it spun him a story of the good life – a college degree en route to a professional, middle-class existence – that made every other alternative less desirable.

However, it's not as though Rob would be the first to fall for that particular story. It's the American Dream: a tale of meritocratic striving where anyone, no matter who they are, can work hard to become a somebody. This is the kind of story that's been told a thousand times and yet still feels fresh. Judging by the runaway success of Broadway musical *Hamilton* since its debut in 2015, a great many of us aren't immune to the appeal of the American Dream.

Write your own deliverance

Like me. I am obsessed with *Hamilton* – even though I admit that its awed reverence for American democratic institutions, ambitious workaholics, verbal dexterity, and unapologetic credentialism makes it the new *West Wing*. Accordingly, I'm trying not to be so smug about my dislike of *Hamilton's* forerunner. (I'm failing miserably.)

The musical narrates the meritocratic rise of Alexander Hamilton. Though a nobody from nowhere, Hamilton's talents, drive, and furious work ethic propel his ascension in the world from illegitimate orphan to American Founding Father. He's an incessant workaholic with a relentless desire to prove his worth. Once Hamilton starts devising the new nation's financial systems as the United States' first secretary of the treasury, he's even more committed to his work. For instance, when his wife Eliza complains that unlike his colleague John Adams, Hamilton doesn't take time off work to spend with family, he scoffs that the office of vice-president isn't exactly a job requiring real effort.

Hamilton's snarky attitude always makes me laugh,

but it also sums up why I love this show and yet feel a great deal of ambivalence about the story Hamilton lives by. Hamilton's obsession with work and effortful striving sweeps aside everything else in its path. Work is central to Hamilton's identity, meaning, and purpose. More than that, work is Hamilton's salvation.

Hamilton exalts what Derek Thompson calls 'workism': work as religion demanding worship and sacrifice. I would call it, naturally, achievement addiction, in light of Jung's claim that addiction is a misdirected yearning for God. Whether religion or addiction, workism is the pursuit of ultimate meaning and satisfaction through achievement. This should be familiar territory for us: secular monks and fictional violin prodigies, who we met in Chapter 3, know a thing or two about work as striving for significance.

The crux is that work becomes all-important, and so holds the keys to someone's happiness and fulfilment. Thompson should know: he confesses he's a 'workist' himself. Or, in our terms, an achievement addict:

> I am devoted to my job. I feel most myself when I am fulfilled by my work – including the work of writing an essay about work. My sense of identity is so bound up in my job, my sense of accomplishment, and my feeling of productivity that bouts of writer's block can send me into an existential funk that can spill over into every part of my life.

This is something every other workist/achievement addict can identify with: in becoming the grounds of intrinsic worth and satisfaction, work morphs into something else too – the ever-present possibility of spiritual crisis. Of all people, I should know: I wrote this little book on it, and rode the highs and lows of everything I've been talking about.

When your identity is at one with your work, any failure to achieve can be soul-destroying because your reason for existence has judged you and found you wanting. And it's not as though you ever really feel satisfied with your achievements. Instead, you need to keep challenging yourself to prove that any success wasn't a one-off. Not only does this set you up to feel permanently insecure, but it provides no solid basis for identity that can withstand the shocks of life: a change of circumstances, losing your job, unexpected illness, or even simply retirement.

But perhaps the biggest challenge facing the workist is that, in the end, it's their responsibility to prove their worth and, effectively, save themselves. In a meritocracy, your fate is ultimately in your hands. Undoubtedly, this makes success pretty sweet (if only briefly). But if you fail, it's hard not to come to a logical, if punishing conclusion: you just didn't have what it takes to thrive.

Meritocracy meets its match

That's the meritocratic story of life. It's no exaggeration to describe it as oppressive since it divides the world into deserving winners and undeserving losers – and declares that everyone got what was coming to them. This is 'the tyranny of merit', as Michael Sandel puts it.

But even if we live within this meritocratic story, it's still just a story – and stories can be out-narrated.

There's a story Jesus told that undermines everything we believe about achievement. Even if religion is not your thing, it's worth comparing the stories we live by with those of a more heavenly bent. At the very least, stories of the second kind help us imagine an alternative to the status quo.

In the New Testament Gospel of Matthew, Jesus tells a story to illustrate the upside-down nature of heaven where 'the last will be first, and the first will be last':

> For the kingdom of heaven is like a landowner who went out early in the morning to hire workers for his vineyard. He agreed to pay them a denarius for the day and sent them into his vineyard.

> About nine in the morning he went out and saw others standing in the marketplace doing nothing. He told them, 'You also go and work in my vineyard, and I will pay you whatever is right.' So they went.

> He went out again about noon and about three in the afternoon and did the same thing. About five in the afternoon he went out and found still others standing around. He asked them, 'Why have you been standing here all day long doing nothing?'

> 'Because no one has hired us,' they answered.

He said to them, 'You also go and work in my vineyard.'

When evening came, the owner of the vineyard said to his foreman, 'Call the workers and pay them their wages, beginning with the last ones hired and going on to the first.'

The workers who were hired about five in the afternoon came and each received a denarius. So when those came who were hired first, they expected to receive more. But each one of them also received a denarius. When they received it, they began to grumble against the landowner. 'These who were hired last worked only one hour,' they said, 'and you have made them equal to us who have borne the burden of the work and the heat of the day.'

But he answered one of them, 'I am not being unfair to you, friend. Didn't you agree to work for a denarius? Take your pay and go. I want to give the one who was hired last the same as I gave you. Don't I have the right to do what I want with my own money? Or are you envious because I am generous?'

So the last will be first, and the first will be last

(Matthew 20:1–16).

It's a killer last line, one that reverses all our expectations. In Jesus the storyteller, meritocracy meets its match. The meritocratic values we consider all-important – like hard work paying off, and earn-ing our way in the world – just do not weigh with God, Jesus says.

Which, if I'm honest, outrages me. *It's just so unfair.* As an achievement addict, I know exactly how those disgruntled workers feel. I want to be recognised for my hard work, and I count being recognised as getting a reward that's consistent with my efforts. But in God's economy, it seems, no one deserves more or less on the basis of how hard or long they toil. The same pay – the same grace, in religious speak – is freely available to all.

More than that, the conventional ways we recognise people's contributions – like high pay, a glowing performance review, or even just good feedback – don't rate a mention in Jesus' story. Which doesn't mean that God undervalues hard work. Only the kind, it seems, that feeds the superiority complex of hard-core strivers who want to set themselves apart from others on the basis of their strenuous efforts. Smug, in other words, is in Jesus' sights.

Which means that the story also undermines the competitiveness that destroys communal bonds. Greater rewards may motivate harder, better work, but they can also fuel the status games we play with each other. As Christian writer C.S. Lewis once observed, pride is essentially competitive: 'Pride gets no pleasure out of having something, only out of having more of it than the next man … It is the comparison that makes you proud: the pleasure of being above the rest.' Yet in this story, each worker is treated with radical equality, leaving no basis for anyone to feel better than anyone else.

In Jesus' story, all our assumptions get overturned.

Beloved community

Let me clarify, at this point, that it's doubtful that Jesus is proposing a utopian economic policy in this story. But it's worth musing on what might be possible if a community made this their story to live by.

Because throughout this little book, I've considered the fruits, so to speak, of the meritocratic tree – or the way people come to reflect the priorities and demands of the system they're in.

It's pretty grim. When people make themselves in the image of a world obsessed with achievement, they become human capital developers, ATARs on legs, walking and talking résumés, gritty Asians (both actual and honorary), Deresiewicz's 'excellent sheep', anxious and insecure high-achievers, and secular monks striving for their own salvation. It also makes sense to pit ourselves against each other, which entrenches bitter divides between hard-working overachievers winning at life, and an underclass of the bitter, resentful, and aggrieved who've been judged to have failed miserably at it.

But a world that better reflected Jesus' vision would be a beloved community – one not roiled by resentment or arrogance on the basis of merit, but marked by a sense of shared fate and belonging.

The apostle Paul calls such a beloved community the 'body of Christ'. This is a body whose members are diverse and varied, but bound together by common cause, mutual love, and concern. To picture the ideal community, Paul draws on the metaphor of the human body that acts as one being, even if it is made up of different members:

> The eye cannot say to the hand, 'I don't need you!' And the head cannot say to the feet, 'I don't need you!' On the contrary, those parts of the body that seem to be weaker are indispensable, and the parts that we think are less honorable we treat with special honour.

(1 Corinthians 12:21–23)

Paul's vision of bodily integrity offers a striking contrast to the unequal status of Head, Heart, and Hand work that David Goodhart identifies in contemporary societies. The meritocratic economy gives special honour to intellectual or white-collar work, while blue-collar (manual labor, basic jobs) and (often) pink-collar employment (the work of care) are invariably diminished. The result is, shall we say, Big Head – which also names the spiritual condition that Head workers are prone to!

Yet Paul's vision checks the excesses of Big Head by remembering that the human body/community is not complete without all its constituent parts. In this community, Head, Heart, and Hand would not be pitted against each other for esteem and rewards.

Instead, each would be honoured for its unique contribution to the common good.

Indeed, so deep is the sense of belonging in the body of Christ that 'If one part suffers, every part suffers with it; if one part is honoured, every part rejoices with it' (1 Corinthians 12:26). This is the kind of human community that Jesus' story of the workers in the vineyard points to: one of shared purpose and fellow feeling despite any individual differences or dissimilar levels of ability.

In this picture of the beloved community, Paul is not prescribing a cure for our current meritocratic ills. But he offers a provocative social vision that counters the way we prioritise achievement above all else. Far from diminishing achievement, Paul simply requires it to be put in the service of others.

What luck to be alive

But perhaps the most profound shift that Jesus' story requires is a change of focus. Meritocracy and an achievement-addicted culture require self-absorption. Both keep our focus on what we do, and how hard we work, in order to rise in the world. That's why some of the workers in Jesus' story are so dissatisfied: they're convinced that they're owed more money for having labored the longest and hardest. But the owner of the vineyard flummoxes them all: 'Don't I have the right to do what I want with my own money? Or are you envious because I am generous?'

It's a reply that dares to suggest that the meritocratic mentality – that hard work leads inexorably to
success – misses something critical: the fact that, ultimately, everything in life is a gift that no one did anything to deserve. So whatever we thought we'd won
for ourselves would prove no match for all that we'd
already received. That understanding alone would
restrain our tendency to get high on our individual
efforts. Instead, our instinct would be gratitude, not a
self-oriented, easily wounded pride.

Which is something that, strangely enough, we can
also intuit in *Hamilton*. As we've already explored, the
musical preaches the virtues of hard work, coupled
with restless ambition, in order to make something
of yourself in the world. Yet one character upends
the show's meritocratic mentality in a dramatic way:
Eliza, Hamilton's wife.

This is a surprise because as a character, Eliza
seems deprived of agency. She may get the guy, but
she's not exactly your typical heroine; her spunky
sister Angelica seems to better fit that bill. Moreover,
Eliza's recurring musical motif stresses her helplessness – in the face of Hamilton's considerable charms,
as well as her futile attempts to get him to stop working. She's passive, which is perhaps the worst thing
you can be in a meritocratic system that casts you
back on your grit and smarts.

But when – spoiler alert! – Hamilton cheats on
Eliza, he discovers that Eliza possesses an unusual
power – one that, despite all her reputed helplessness,

he cannot claim by force, or earn through strenuous effort. It's the power of forgiveness, which leaves him at the mercy of this most passive of characters. Hamilton may deserve Eliza's blame and resentment, but she offers him a gift of grace he knows he isn't worthy of.

Eliza, by the way, seems highly attuned to grace. While she's a big believer in Hamilton's talents, she resists the idea that he needs to work non-stop to secure his legacy. Eliza frequently reminds him to take in the marvel of being alive at all. She doesn't mean that he should stop striving altogether – but that he should stop every once in a while and remember that life itself is a miracle.

We have much to learn from Eliza's way of seeing things. She reminds us of what really matters in the end, and also what preceded all our striving in the first place. I can't believe I'm saying this, but maybe it wouldn't hurt for achievement addicts like myself to adopt something of Eliza's helplessness. You never know: leaning into the luckiness of existence, or recognising the givenness of all things, might nurture in us a desire to give thanks.

All of us live storied lives. If the picture we get in Jesus' story of the workers in the vineyard is a picture of ultimate reality, then Eliza's instinct for gratitude is far more in tune with that reality than the way the rest of us are constantly striving for our significance.

Having lived far too long in a story where life comes down to grit, I'm leaning into the one that reminds me what matters infinitely more: gift.

Re:CONSIDERING

CODA

This little book has been excruciating to write, but inadvertently therapeutic. While reading Christina Ho, Alice Pung, and Amy Chua's various chronicles of Asian achievement addiction, I have laughed, groaned, cursed, and winced in horrified recognition – and mourned the human cost of it all. I also found William Deresiewicz an excellent shepherd to 'excellent sheep'.

I also took the opportunity to borrow a practice from AA: to take responsibility and apologise for the ways my achievement addiction might have hurt others. Remember that girl I was mean to when I was 18? I didn't have to search far and wide to, as I've heard in various self-help seminars over the years, 'complete' or reconcile with her. She's been my best friend for over 20 years.

She remembered The Incident when I recently brought it up with her. I asked her why she would have wanted to be friends with such a mean, anxious grade-grubber.

She simply said that she had a sense of the pressure that was on me and didn't judge me for it.

At some point after that day, we became friends – I can't exactly remember how. But it was probably her kindness that kicked it all off.

We believe very different things about the world. But I can't help feeling that the grace she showed me was also a glimpse of the grace of God. The kind that can't be earned, but only received with grateful thanks.

I am so grateful. For in a world obsessed with merit, grace is just miraculous.

Re: CONSIDERING

NOTES

INTRODUCTION

Page 3: addiction may be just as much a spiritual affliction. Having said that, if you or someone you know is experiencing addiction in the medical sense, please seek help from a medical professional. That's not me.

Page 3: Jung stuck a Bible verse in a footnote. The link between Carl Jung and Alcoholics Anonymous is cited widely on the internet, but you can also chase up this letter at https://barricks.com/AASayings/BillW_CarlJung_Letters.pdf

Page 4: ask journalist Barbara Ehrenreich. Barbara Ehrenreich, *Smile or Die: How Positive Thinking Fooled America and The World* (Granta, London, 2009).

Page 4: see also Rhonda Byrne's self-help sensation. Rhonda Byrne, *The Secret* (Atria Books, New York, 2006).

Page 5: the way we mark significant life milestones. Clare Thorp writes about this fascinating trend in 'Mid-life Crisis, Gen-X-Style: Less Running Away, More Running Marathons', published 31 July 2020 in *The Sydney Morning Herald Good Weekend*.

Page 6: 'We are a nation of lifters, not leaners'. An abridged transcript of Joe Hockey's budget speech was published 14 May 2014 in the *Australian Financial Review*.

Page 9: following in her schooling steps. She's given permission for me to reveal that she used to be a bit of a bottler-upper, so I'm not exactly saying that piano was where she exorcised her angst. But I'm not *not* saying that either.

1. STRIVE

Page 11: 'They run the tests through a machine'. Alice Pung, 'The Secret Life of Them', *Close to Home: Selected Writings* (Black Inc. Books, Carlton, 2018), p. 207.

Page 12: academic striving has superseded athletic ambition. This unnerving spectacle was reported on by Jordan Baker and Sarah Keoghan in '"It Felt Like a Real Exam": Over 1000 Kids Take a Break from Summer Holidays', published 13 January 2019 in *The Sydney Morning Herald*.

Page 12: take a guess what background might heavily feature in the crowd? As cited in Christina Ho, *Aspiration and Anxiety: Asian Migrants and Australian Schooling* (Melbourne University Press, Carlton, 2020), p. 68. Ho cites another article as the source of this claim: Alison Broinowski,

'Unnatural Selection', published 24 January 2015 in *The Sydney Morning Herald Good Weekend*.

Page 13: I'd be crazy to rush in where the white woke fear to tread. Which, in case you were wondering, doesn't necessarily license non-Asians to talk so flippantly about such matters. Also, thank you to NM for the language of the 'white woke'.

Page 13: They – we – are people of grit. It does not surprise me at all that Chinese-American psychologist Angela Duckworth wrote The Book on grit – or the idea that passion and perseverance, rather than natural talent, are the secret to success. Duckworth is herself living proof of her thesis. In her foreword, she recalls that when she was a child, her dad would often remark that she was 'no genius'. A few decades later, however, Duckworth was awarded a prestigious MacArthur Fellowship – commonly known as a 'genius grant' – for her work showing that there were no inherent advantages to being gifted. Forget Cinderella getting to marry her prince – Duckworth's story is the kind of fairytale that I wish someone had told me when I was young. See Angela Duckworth, *Grit: Why Passion and Resilience are the Secrets to Success* (Penguin Random House, London, 2016).

Page 13: 'My goal as a parent'. Amy Chua, *Battle Hymn of the Tiger Mother* (Bloomsbury, London, 2011), p. 49.

Page 14: stressed-out six-year-old. Chua, *Battle Hymn of the Tiger Mother*, p. 59.

Page 14: 'went to recess instead of doing extra credit'. Original emphasis, Chua, *Battle Hymn of the Tiger Mother*, p. 68.

Page 14: run around during lunch time. Daniel Markovits, *The Meritocracy Trap: How America's Foundational Myth Feeds Inequality, Dismantles the Middle Class, and Devours the Elite* (Penguin, London, 2019), p. 39.

Page 14: everyone knows a 'white tiger parent'. You can check out Sharon Verghis' take on 'white tiger parenting' in an article published on 20 January 2020 for SBS.

Page 15: 'this is NOT the A-League'. At playbytherules.net.au you can download a template of a sign you might want to take to weekend matches.

Page 15: 'If you think that you have worked hard'. Peggy Liddick's full letter is available through Chip Le Grand's 9 May 2021 article 'Cruel Game: Former Gymnasts Open Up on Culture of Fear and Control', published in *The Sydney Morning Herald*.

Page 16: an extreme version of 'concerted cultivation'. Annette Lareau, *Unequal Childhoods: Class, Race, and Family Life* (University of California Press, Berkeley, 2011).

Page 17: grooms kids for bougie, professional life. See Joe Pinsker's article '"Intensive Parenting" Is Now the Norm in America' in *The Atlantic*, published 17 January 2019.

Page 18: Lowy Institute survey of Chinese-Australians. You can check out the Lowy Institute survey at https://charts.lowyinstitute.org/features/chinese-communities/

Page 19: go so far as to ban TV. Ho, *Aspiration and Anxiety*, pp. 79–82.

Page 19: people with surnames like yours. Ho, *Aspiration and Anxiety*, p. 19.

Page 19: 'I don't really have time for anything fun'. Chua, *Battle Hymn of the Tiger Mother*, p. 67.

Page 20: I don't want this number to define who I am. Eden was featured in James Maasdorp's article 'Is Year 12 Worth It? High School Students Battle Pressures after Self-documenting Final Year', published 20 February 2017 by the ABC.

Pages 20–21: work mentality of 'millennial burnout'. Anne Helen Petersen, *Can't Even: How Millennials Became the Burnout Generation* (Vintage, London, 2021).

Page 21: designation of 'excellent sheep'. William Deresiewicz, *Excellent Sheep: The Miseducation of the American Elite and the Way to a Meaningful Life* (Free Press, New York, 2015).

Page 22: status-obsessed Sydney. Bri Lee, *Who Gets to Be Smart: Privilege, Power and Knowledge* (Allen & Unwin, Crows Nest, 2021), p. 30.

2. SUFFER

Page 24: no shower necessary. Jia Tolentino, 'Always Be Optimising', *Trick Mirror: Reflections on Self-Delusion* (4th Estate, London, 2019), p. 76.

Page 26: 'sore feet and aching hips.' Pauline was featured in Sadie Nicholas' article '10K Steps a Day', published 30 July 2020 in *The Daily Mail*.

Page 27: 'maternity clothing is in storage'. From a March 2021 post from the Instagram account of the legendary 'mama and midwife' Hannah Polites.

Pages 28–29: 'When I had my first business when I was 19'. Tim was featured in Sam Levin's article 'Millionaire Tells Millennials: If You Want a House, Stop Buying Avocado Toast', published 16 May 2017 in *The Guardian*.

Page 29: spoiled brats with lavish tastes. Bernard Salt's column 'Moralisers, We Need You!' was published 15–16 October 2016 in *The Weekend Australian Magazine*.

Page 29: forsake 46,509 avocado toasts. The Avocado Index was published on 25 October 2016 in *The Real Estate Conversation*.

Page 31: 'you feel like you've won'. See 'Excellent Sheep', Life & Faith, https://www.publicchristianity.org/excellent_sheep/

Page 31: 'public display of productivity'. Ben Tarnoff's article 'The New Status Symbol: It's Not What You Spend – It's How Hard You Work' was published 24 April 2017 in *The Guardian*.

Page 31: 'I can do nearly anything'. Catherine Clifford's article 'Billionaire Jack Dorsey's 11 "Wellness" Habits' was published 8 April 2019 on CNBC.

Page 32: Dorsey is a 'secular monk'. Andrew Taggart's article 'Secular Monks' was published March 2020 by *First Things*.

Page 33: 'absence of acclaim for my musicianship'. Jessie Tu, *A Lonely Girl is a Dangerous Thing* (Allen & Unwin, Crows Nest, 2020), p. 31.

Page 33: 'a hole in me that was ultimately unfillable'. Tu, *A Lonely Girl*, p. 125.

Page 34: 'bowl of razor blades'. Tu, *A Lonely Girl*, p. 154.

Page 35: 'I'd stare at myself in the mirror'. Tu, *A Lonely Girl*, p. 121.

3. SMUG

Page 36: 'almost every night before I go to sleep'. Terry was featured in Sarah Lyall's article 'They Can't Get Enough of *The West Wing* Right Now', published 19 December 2019 in *The New York Times*.

Page 38: 'inhale too deeply of their success'. Michael J. Sandel, *The Tyranny of Merit: What's Become of the Common Good?* (Farrar, Straus and Giroux, New York, 2020), p. 24.

Page 39: 'aspirational roadmap for upward mobility'. You can find Rob Henderson's column 'Everything I Know about Elite America I Learned from *Fresh Prince and The West Wing'*, published 10 October 2020 in *The New York Times*.

Page 40: through a university degree. Though part of the experience of 'millennial burnout' is the realisation that a university degree no longer sets you up for a stable job or financial security. See Anne Helen Petersen, *Can't Even*, pp. 45–65.

Page 40: surveys from the United Kingdom, the United States. Sandel, *The Tyranny of Merit*, p. 95.

Pages 40–41: being educated is no guarantee that you won't also be prejudiced. Amy Chua notes that well-educated Americans 'don't see how tribal their cosmopolitanism is', with clear in- and out-groups. Amy Chua, *Political Tribes: Group Instinct and the Fate of Nations* (Bloomsbury, London, 2018). See also Jonathan Haidt, *The Righteous Mind: Why Good People are Divided by Politics and Religion* (Vintage, New York, 2012). On p. 94 Haidt argues that the more education you have, the better you are at generating self-justifying reasons for your actions.

Page 41: 'politics of humiliation'. Sandel, *The Tyranny of Merit*, p. 25.

Page 42: 'the wealth of our middle class'. A transcript of US President Donald Trump's inauguration speech was published on 20 January 2017 on *Politico*.

Page 42: 'forgotten men and women of our country'. See previous note.

Page 43: he wasn't a professional politician. Joan C. Williams' article 'What So Many People Don't Get about the US Working Class' was published 10 November 2016 in *The Harvard Business Review*.

Page 43: tell everyone else how to do their job. Alfred Lubrano quoted in Williams, 'What So Many People Don't Get about the US Working Class'.

Page 43: 'basket of deplorables'. You can see Democratic presidential nominee Hillary Clinton's comments in context in a transcript published 10 September 2016 in *Time*.

Page 43: fend off the dumb. Luke Savage, 'How Liberals Fell in Love with *The West Wing*', published 7 June 2017 in *Current Affairs*.

Page 45: 'Hufflepuff are a lot o' duffers'. J. K. Rowling, *Harry Potter and the Philosopher's Stone* (Bloomsbury, London, 1997), p. 61.

Page 45: 'one form of human aptitude'. Original emphasis, David Goodhart, *Head, Hand, Heart: The Struggle for Dignity and Status in the 21st Century* (Penguin, London, 2020), p. 3.

Page 46: economists who coined the term. Anne Case and Angus Deaton, *Deaths of Despair and the Future of Capitalism* (Princeton University Press, Princeton, 2020).

Page 46: 'A four-year degree'. Case and Deaton, *Deaths of Despair and the Future of Capitalism*, p. 3.

Page 47: 'somatise the insult'. Markovits, *The Meritocracy Trap*, p. 61.

4. STORY TIME

Page 49: 'The universe is made of stories, not of atoms'. Muriel Rukeyser, 'The Speed of Darkness', *The Collected Poems of Muriel Rukeyser* (University of Pittsburgh Press, Pittsburgh PA, 2005), p. 467.

Page 51: what Derek Thompson calls 'workism'. Derek Thompson's article 'Workism Is Making Americans Miserable' was published 24 February 2019 in *The Atlantic*.

Page 51: 'I am devoted to my job'. See previous note.

Page 55: 'Pride gets no pleasure out of having something'. C.S. Lewis, *Mere Christianity* (Macmillan, New York, 1943), pp. 109–110.

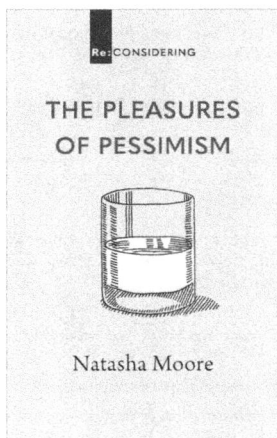

Pandemic, supervolcano, late capitalism, transhumanism, populism, cancel culture, the post-antibiotic age, the gig economy, the surveillance state, the cascading effects of climate change …

Whatever the specifics, do you feel like things have gone off the rails – or are just about to?

If you've read the news, watched a zombie movie, or gotten into an argument on Twitter lately, the answer is probably yes.

And you're not alone.

What makes us such apocaholics?

What's so appealing about Armageddon? What are the pleasures – and also the perils – of our pessimism?

ALSO AVAILABLE

Who's in favour of compassion?

Pretty much everybody, actually.

Left or right, religious or not, nobody seems to have a bad word to say about compassion.

So why do we have so much trouble addressing the conflict, inequality, and suffering in our world?

Ranging from the streets of St Kilda to the slums of Delhi, from Plato to Nietzsche, the Dalai Lama to Peter Singer, and from *Seinfeld* to the Good Samaritan, Tim Costello appeals to our common humanity – and takes an unflinching look at how costly compassion can be.

ALSO AVAILABLE

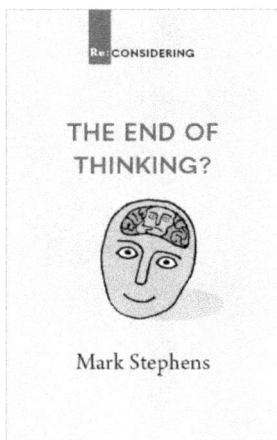

THE END OF THINKING?

Mark Stephens

What were you thinking?

We all feel entitled to our opinion. Whether it be our take on politics, vaccines, parenting, or the value of religion, everybody wants to have their say - and everybody loves to be right.

But do we know what it means to think well?

Covering 'idiot brain', lobotomies, the difference between certainty and confidence, the nature of facts, and the virtue of intellectual hospitality, Mark Stephens invites you to consider not just what you think but how and why you think.

Do we think only for ourselves, or also for the good of others?

www.ingramcontent.com/pod-product-compliance
Lightning Source LLC
Chambersburg PA
CBHW060037050426
42448CB00012B/3052